ON

(

.

subaqueous press

ACKNOWLEDGMENTS

Grateful acknowledgment is made to the following publications in which some of these poems first appeared:

The Amicus Journal, ONTHEBUS, 4th Street, The Crab Creek Review, Poetry Bone, PoetsWest, synapse, Whispering into the Wind

ISBN 0-9724836-0-8
Library of Congress Control Number 2002094909

FIRST EDITION

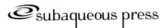subaqueous press

3213 West Wheeler Street #304
Seattle, Washington 98199
206.781.3881
subaqueouspress@attbi.com
www.lunacydewpoint.com

Cover art by Kathryn Klein
Cover design and layout by Matt Coppins – www.mattcoppins.com
Printed on acid-free paper
Manufactured in the United States of America

CONTENTS

ON THE DREAMING EARTH

WHILE YOU SLEPT

Kicked up from nowhere, kicked up from sleep
and splintered by rain
the reckless wind slings away our voices.
On the beach we bear the brunt of the change
in feverish sleep by the churning sand
with the questions gusting through the slats
of every fence in the neighborhood.
The wind gets in me like a spirit,
scattering things, whisking through the locks,
roughing up the surf,
listening to no voice.
Shh, I want to tell you about it —

BODY OF WATER

The cool sheets, the hours swimming past,
the clock's measured voice yes no yes no, dreams
rising to the surface.
The steady room
embraced by darkness,
a patient sheen at the window's edge, and
Sleep will come, Sleep will come say the unseen
white walls, edging toward the window
all dissolving

                Fish swimming toward the light

I GOT UP AND WALKED LIKE A GHOST

through my own empty rooms.
I was wearing some garment that only showed up
in moonlight, I was
sliding across the floorboards trailing
a spectral hem, thinking

> *Life is short and desires are so long.*
> *A hand, reaching from a world apart,*
> *Caresses and arouses this fire-cold heart.*
> *I'll pace these rooms until I meet the dawn.*

Ghost Girl treads my floors while I
lie listless and empty of any dream
because she has gotten up and gone from me,
is smoking out the window, her flashing eye fixed
on the places that can't be reached
from where we are.
When I sleep she walks;
she never sleeps;
sometimes we two meet
and my eyes in their hollows
see through things,
and I don't recognize my name or my life
until she withdraws back into my core
and lets me mend in sleep.

MYSTERY KISS

You are an angel that fell
and you fell into the lake of my dreams.
It must have been during the night
while I was making my somnambulist rounds,
my mind a bowl half full of water
into which you dropped like a cut flower,
my body, as always, not temple, but vessel,
your voice pouring into me
with the liquid whisper of steam,
the touch of lips
not a seal
but the brush of wind
as a door opening on all that's within
swings open

WOMAN IN THE POOL

Nothing matches the silent aquamarine
for a medium to move in:
lap after lap, breathless voices glancing off
the high brick walls, unbreathable water
sliding past my nostrils. Blue microcosm.

From the opposite direction I approach the swimmer in the
    next lane.
As we pass
she mistakenly strokes my arm, languidly,
lingering with body-temperature smooth
fingers.
Where is your grasp,
unknown caress?
Through the blue slides my body,
my arm with the one spot now that trembles.

TOMBOY

Her hands are covered in sand and there is sand
stuck up the leg hole of her bathing suit
all gritty up near her little closed pussy.
Her hair is all salty. It's her weird parents who
make her do weird stuff,
actually she's adopted she says,
she came in with the flotsam and that's what
makes her so hardy.
She gambols off with a toss
of her head, all swinging
arms, and leggy.

Standing up on the high
concrete dock, several times her height above the water,
she looks so slight
it seems it would take her a long time to fall
through the resistant air
but the fact is
when those scrubby toes push her tomboy body weight
up off the edge
she describes a quick arc
in the late summer
quickly toward the water,
her skin milky under the ruddy suntan,
her shape growing regardless of the ill-fitting
swimsuit, salty hair flying
eyes squeezed shut, sun glistening on the
endless wave as it receives her,
she's heading for the ocean floor but
the water will catch her like a net she's
plunging in the sea bird flying over
calls out *Surrender!*
and the tough little soles of her feet
are the last to go under.

SOLUTIO

Little fish, surrounded by water, you slip in my grasp.
When I dove I was thinking *Pearl*... or
How long can I hold my breath —
but what I came to was
the shut water, and you,
wriggling between my hands,
separated from the whole school
of thoughts you run with
together without a language —
Fish you are
a secret creature
darting through the shadowy sea,
as soon here as gone, effortlessly,
whereas me, I may go ahead and dip
my body in, or even go way
deep
down
but can never glide there like you
who contain the sea within you
and can never drown.

FEMALE'S DREAM OF A MALE DREAMING OF BEING FEMALE

He pushed aside her panties
to taste it for himself.
They lay where the sand was waiting for the wave.
The grittiness against their skin
reminded them of the earth
turning in space, and put them in their place
with love
and sex — oh,
sex.

Opening her legs to his mouth
was a gesture of the ages.
Her scent bound them to the earth.
That was when the wave came in.

With the wave in came the secrets of the sea
and they lay
awash in secrets, she on her back
facing the sky, he with his cool face
between her thighs,
right there at the center of the universe.

CUTTING INTO THE COCONUT

The ocean takes bites out of Tutu Bay
and spits them back onto the beach, where he makes his home.
Banana trees and mango

lean back in the breeze.
The hut, the hammock, an old and
cracked red board lying in the sparse grass:

this is all.
Rainfall is scarce, but knowing
another source, he yanks

the rusted machete from the stump,
squats down and rolls a coconut onto the board.
Turning the husk with a dark sandy hand

he hacks off one end, pulls away the fibrous green skin
and digs a finger into the fruit.
At the sound of liquid sloshing inside he tilts back his head

and drinks, sticky milk running down his upturned chin,
throat working as he swallows the whole
carnivorous ocean from that one sweet seed.

ARRIVAL

Cobblestone street toils up the steep slope
twisting between the stone houses in the
bitch heat of the afternoon,
old, old way, always trapped and craving.

But when you round the last turn of the village at
once the plateau stretches out before you,
out to the swimming clouds in the blue, and there
is the unfurled road
making for the horizon.

Green farmland rolls out into the valleys below,
quenching the dirt,
lush as the tongue lying
in the mouth without speaking,
this mouth of a world.

SLEEPING OUT IN TUTU BAY

The moon is in a big hurry, and long before the sun is down
the moon sails up
because night just can't wait so near the tropics
where the day sleeps in the sun without dreaming
but in the dark the world begins to throb:
Palm trees wave lusty fronds
in a slow frenzy against the bright dark sky,
and drenched in salt and moonlight, the air
is for breathing in, and in, and who can sleep?
Look, see how the evening is glittering?
I want to swallow it whole, but it swallows me:
my blood singing through my body, the stars
pulsing in a jet black sky the stars
falling to the beach and staining the earth with desire.

WHITE ROSE

The white rose bloomed in the dark
while you unbuttoned my dress
in the near-rain
on the deserted street, wide
and deserted as the palm of your hand
before I press myself against it.

The white rose bloomed in the grey dawn
as we looked but did not touch
each other
and looked with the hunger
of our whole lives.

The white rose blooming
at the garden wall couldn't
help but bloom
as the light in the garage clicked off
and your hands found me
and I turned into a woman all over again.

White rose bloomed
while the hurricane passed through
arousing the petals with droplets
arousing its fragrance
You kissed me

White rose bloomed while your hands
traveled over me
in the unrecognizable evening
while you climbed up me and I forswore
my world
We stepped outside to smell the rose
as it bloomed

and as it bloomed you missed your flight
and missed your flight
I heard you call my name
I begged you to let me
The sirens screamed round us
I barely dreamed for lack of sleep but dreamed
the earth quaked
Maybe that was what knocked
the first petal loose

White rose kept blooming into the next moment
and after you were gone
a million years
at dusk I saw the wind
pick off the second to last white petal
I burn to see you

WAVE-PARTICLE DUALITY

Dawn came like a ghost into the huge black
bowl of night, and across the black
wind-flogged bay, where a lunatic wind
worked as if it could derange
the light, which nothing could upset.
I slept while it blew.

Dawn came from the imagination to Cascade Bay,
stole over my marrow,
spectral messenger
of change,
while I slept.

Dawn came in the causal
world to the wind
which howled like any love-starved soul,
forced entry at the chimney,
battered at the pressure.
Night the amnesiac still rocked me in my bed.

Dawn bloomed like the sudden remembrance of a dream.
I woke to the hysterical wind, the icy bay
and my lover beside me still rapt in the pictures passing
        between his eyes and fluttering eyelids.
Deeper than deeper than the chafing wind
a big, slow door
silently opened.
Day crowded the doorway,
the ghost was gone

FOOL'S JOURNEY

I knew a boy well who nearly found me
without my finding
him first,
magical
half of the self
that he was.
It started with water
free as a gift in the short grass,
muddy, precious, glimpsed
and lost
along the wet ridge between the swamps
where everything looked familiar but the way
was not there,
and finished with water.

I looked further afield,
caught the bus that rode along the edge
of the sea
as evening spilled into the swells
and with all my feminine charms
I pressed that wiry little shuttle-bus driver —
who threaded the shoreline through his eyes
day after endlessly linked day,
like Charon never disembarking,
knowing the route without knowing an ending
but knowing —
and I got him to tell me
If you find it in the inner streets around
the dark avenue that used to be the river
that fell into this sea

don't be surprised.
Well I looked in the city.
Time and place
had run over that river indeed:
I tried all the alleys, culverts, steam grates and so on,

strained to hear it gurgling in the concrete,
but the city has so many hiding places
I searched in vain.

Older still and by the same sea,
I walked along a sun-stunned beach,
a young and lovely belle
with a belle I loved.
We flowed along the vestigial sand together, my arm wound
    around her,
and I'll never forget her curvingly
perfect hipbone
nestled against my lifeline
as I promised
her the hidden water
that sprung unasked from the ground, and knew I had her.

But as I drew her with me instinctively toward that spot
the swamps rose from the sand,
the brackish, thickening water
swimming with flotsam rose to claim us
and we struggled in that tide of vengeance
with its shifting floor —
until I propelled us out of there just barely,
then watched the angry marsh sweep past us,
the fountain
now altogether improbable in that light.
I lost her.

After years of trying to appease those currents
and finally learning to be lost
I found myself wandering through the empty streets of some
ancient empty afternoon
and I met a young boy just emerging from the world:
He had no path, he had
sprung from the soil

and as he leaned close to brush my ear
with the breath of the words of his secret wish
I closed my eyes to hear the inside of the words
and of course it turned into a kiss:
It was the heat of his youth turned inside out
into my mouth and all of that fire
sending up into my veins as up a flue
and I that fire-hungry
passage the stoked heat
dissipated into —

and then I was crouching here,
scooping up drinkable water
in an initialled cup,
and nothing to say so, just the almost invisible
spring everywhere beneath us:
the veins of the grimy streets,
foundation of the transient sand,
medium for the delicate love
of the flesh, tidal pull of the unknown,
known,
unknown.

WHAT, THEN

I want
something sweet
but not
so sweet
as the bite
into thick-skinned
almost black
wild fat
grape off the wild vine
by the dirt road in August.
I was nine.
Not quite that.

I want something
sweet but
not so sweet it
burns my tongue
and throat and makes
me feel
that's the last time
I eat that.

I want something sweet but
not that
sweet baby
in fact
don't give me any sweet at all right now,
just mean and true,
no sweetness now but
for that slim edge of what
it'll feel like later
when we're through.

I want something sweet, by now
I know that
much but what

else I know is sweetness
disappears
like a star directly
gazed upon
if you touch it
with the wrong
part of the tongue.

I want something sweet so badly I'm
perpetually craving chocolate,
dark
chocolate,
trying to savor
my way
to the bitterness at its
heart,
bitter
in the sweet,
dark, dark
deep-down
realm of Pluto
where riches luxuriate,
under
the dragon's paw:
Take them up
on the tongue:
Dark,
so sweet.

I want something sweet because
surely sweetness will fill the void.

I
want
something
sweet

you see,
inside
and out,
transforming
all
bitterness
that's gone
before,
all doubt
and weariness
gone,
sweet
beyond
flavor,
beyond
memory
or meaning,
just
past
dying,
when

SOUL-PICTURE

I'm lying alone in this
big wide bed
There's a desert on my right
a desert on my left
The foot slopes off into
        oblivion

At the center of the bed is my perfect cunt
From the head of the bed the ancestors gaze down
        to where my mind wanders away
My feet point south as if to slice into the abyss first
        without leaving a ripple
My arms are free to roam and steal
and cop a feel off my own soul

I have slithered across this bed on my belly
to make a man follow me with one
purpose,
where all we did
was all there was

A rumble of thunder and the ions change
Then the rain falls, leaves droop

Shiva's still dancing,
and I'm only as good as
the last time I did it

BODY OF WOMAN

In my imagination your shoulders blur
like wings, slender
feet flashing like
little fish, you are
flying and I'm burning
See my mind is full of pictures
but with you lying beneath me
my soul spilling over you like milk
the room sliding in every direction
your body is only
Love's beast after all, Love's
blood beating, and solid
as I am
but with your yielding
yielding
my yielding
an uroboros forms
with no opposite
force there to stop us
from eddying inward
to where your belly button the old
scar
reminds us
divides us
back into our separate skins
I lean back so I can see you again
I see you again
Swim into me body of woman

SISTER SELF

As we descend it becomes
darker
I can feel the darkness in my bowels
The high heels
that keep me a few inches above the ground of
space & time
are useless to me now
I'm calling out
for my sister to join me, I'm weeping her name
As her face appears
inside my face I can
name my tears, one by one
on their way down:
one that glistens even in the dark,
one that's shed like the old luggage of a snake,
one that came from nowhere, into nowhere
one that's torn from the reservoir inside
formed from crying into crying
and the last long tear, sliding down while the first one
is still drying
Down
down
A hissing in my ears
For all the times I flew now I'm making this
descent
I listen with my inner ear, arbiter of balance,
the dark opens out of me
into soft gigantic petals
At the blossom's black center
I entwine
fingers with
my familiar
and unrecognizable
sister

LINES WRITTEN AFTER WE FINALLY ADDRESSED EACH OTHER BY NAME

They came up from many stories underground, the unknown
    men,
to knock at my door carrying black suitcases
and when I asked them
what they had for me
their faces disappeared beneath their hats
Magritte style and that was that.
Later I dreamed of you.
I was awake then, and
next to me in the blue
room on the blue cloud
bed breathed
the intractable memory of you
with a badge of honor worn over the spot
where I had listened for your heart
to see how hard it beat for me.
And last night
while in flight you drank yourself into the emptiness
at the tips of your fingers, my name
on your lips
and everything you knew gone forever gone gone
and the arrow driving
deeper into your heart where you had
let down your guard,
I raging paced out this maddening maze and the thing is
even in a maze you follow only
one path, though it seems like many.

As the sun goes
down tonight may I take
nothing for granted,
may the contents of those suitcases be
revealed to me,
may I feel

your breath in my mouth again, your cock hard against me
    again,
may this endless flame that burns in my veins
instead of blood so that I am like
the torch you hold, may it purify
as fire does
and may I feel you within me always.

ON DESOLATION SOUND

I fell in love on Desolation Sound.
It was because the water was so still, it was
the uncertain depth, and I fell.
The feeling of falling
was like the wind waiting in the trees
or the islands, great sleeping beasts,
dreaming of emergence from their supine shores.
Wet dirt, wet grass, pines drenched with my own longing,
pines bending toward the water
as one.

I fell
when the wind plucked its way across the water, I fell
slowly and deliberately, I fell
and kept falling in the long grass.
I fell under the red madrona trees, ancient with longing, I fell
when your fingers touched my throat, and kept falling.

Somewhere else the ferries churned, voices sounded across
the expanse
but under the trees at the still point, with your
breath in my mouth, on the dreaming earth,
I found myself turning to stone,
then to wind, then to water, then to flesh.
I was all these things in your arms
in the stillness
while the day kept falling right through us,
through the trees, through the windows and walls,
through the still water shivering in my limbs and
                                    everywhere.

I fell
when at dusk the cold wind opened my face again, fell
when my shadow lengthened across the wide field
and joined me with the evening,
fell with the sharp light disappearing across everything we
                            could see.

I fell in love on Desolation Sound,
it was at your exact touch
with your voice slipping into my veins
in the undivided silence in the dark and I fell
and kept falling

PAIN HONEYMOON

1st day:
Electrified with wonder we lay clasped without moving
in that hotel room with the window beating in the wind
and I wondered until I could feel you burning
in every pore of my skin.
I have lain with you now while the fog crept in
and I have felt a certain light
enter my soul and make room.

2nd day:
So we risk everything under a starless
sky all words and no meaning
got my hook in your mouth and it's
too late to swim
away so we try not
to drown in all this.
My heart won't be still and the night will not stop.
I face the morning with fear
from my side of the bed.
In the dark we say dark things, you said.

3rd day:
In the all-night convenience store
where we've gone at 1:59 A.M. for beer
a man tries to section a girl's apple
for her with a razor blade well he
slices his thumb and bleeds all over the apple
turns out he's the busdriver has to
drive all night long
with this damn thumb now and she
his passenger gives no word of thanks just
a distasteful glance at her bloody
apple well it's fruit for the all-night ride,
and isn't it
the girl's job to open the apple —
and whose job to bleed?

We leave the store in love
and rage, sorrow,
glee, betrayal and promises
promises promises.
The night doesn't get any younger.

4th day:
Now the moon is nearly in the sea.
The warm pouring wind has deserted this place
over and over again.
While you sleep in doubt I look out the open
door at the mist
dragging itself up over the glistening bay
and onto the headland until I
can imagine it with my bare skin
and am revisited by my dream of
the house of fog you and I lived in.
I sit,
and watch,
and wait.
It's when the fog finally enters
and alights on my lashes
that I know it's time to shut the door
and wake you up to carry on
because I've seen the world turn like this before
and the thing is it doesn't turn back.

THE MOON IN THE MAN

Even a careful man may be
     reckless inside.
The headlights streaking through the blackness
     of his imagination may turn upon
strange creatures journeying across the highway
     at that deep hour.
A man may measure his stride to match
     his need; he may
find many ways of approaching a problem, including
     letting it lie.
What lies dormant may be
     just the thing
a woman taps into.
     A man may
rise and set with the sun but still be
     guided all day long
by the progress of the
     undercover moon.
As the Milky Way sparks a steady stream
     just behind his brow
so do the words when he addresses her
     leave his mouth
to say things he can only say
     by saying them to her.
Even the Man in the Moon
     has this mistress
and is ruled from within
     more mysteriously than from without. Man:
Moon will rule you
     from within. (Look out...)

WHAT THE WOMAN SAID

Men are creatures just like us.
Men are the antithesis.
Men are the greener grass.
Men are the ones who fight the wars.
Men are the ones who start the wars.

If women are flowers, men are the dirt.
If women are dirt, men are the rocks.
If women are stone, men are the wind.
If women are rain, men are rain.
(If women are the ocean, men are ships who sail out
thinking the world is flat.)

TALK, TALK

These things keep saying themselves
to me, she confided. I'm like a
fox fur, I can't ever
really sleep.

FOX FUR

It lay around
her shoulders like a man
with insomnia. I keep waiting
for it to speak to her
or to tell me what it dreams
all day long with that faraway look.

WITHOUT THINKING #2

Anything that makes you breathe
is as good as the night
sky in full flower
or roadkill for a jackal.
"Rumble and gasp of the surf"
interrupts nothing.
The jetsam on the shore has been through
the cycle so many times
even Adam has forgotten its name.

WITHOUT THINKING #1

The book falls asleep
beside her head: this is not
a new idea.
There remains the solicitous
question of whether the lines
that sleep between the pages are known
to anyone or whether the rain
just falls because it feels like it.

DROP OF BUDDHA

Every year the rain comes
and tilts the globe a little, changing everything,
and all these changes have become one
transformation, one reservoir of thought,
    a single thought.

Lying awake in the darkness I beg
the rain not to stop,
rain that leeches out the poetry, allowing the electric body to
                                    grow,
that leaves us alone without deserting us,
rain and its many frequencies, falling all through the night,
rain landing on the water
    more water

In the wash of it the present grows dim.
Other regions of the mind explore themselves without our
                                    knowledge.
Fickle memory, one tries to turn
to the senses for the simple truth:
I know that on the many nights in the past (gone yet re-
                                    created)
when I have lain listening to rain
sounding just like this
it sounded just like this.

On the Planet with Liquid Water

Without magic, with only the meagerness of reason
they took the same path they kept losing —
back to the well.
Everywhere they looked, the tears in their eyes
glistened on the hard desert all around.
"Shall we dig," they wondered, when they faced the mirage,
"while we wait for the rain,
that same long path?"

Make Me

Outside the long rain falls
falls
and nothing can stop it
I would like to fall like that
let go of the top and drop down
changing everything:
So much for the way things were
or will be

POEM

Because it is evening.
Because the shadows lengthen until we're on the other side.
Because the moment expires in beauty,
because the earth is not perfectly round, the year
    not exact, and we set the clocks ahead to keep
    up with the orbit,
    orbiting ourselves.
Because I have all the time there is
    to fill these shoes —
    no time at all.
Because I feel the moment enter me
    and expand
    into all time
    with the radio drifting in the window and pinning
    time to nothing.
Because a moment is a word in my mouth behind which
    everything streams.
Because the shadows lengthen
    and the light slides away
       I'm crying in your arms.

WINTER COMES EARLY

Moon sails from the east, fat
and full yellow at the treeline.
In the garden the tomatoes have dropped from the vines,
yellowed and brittle from two killing frosts
and October just broken.

The sun's last rays
cast a few gold ornaments into the bare branches.
Moon hardens, brightens,
steering higher in its inky ocean.

The gardener has unstrung the vines from the poles.
His footprints are frozen
between the rows, the ridged tread
iced over.
Red peasant grass pokes through the thin
layer of snow, rusting the field.
The house has turned its back
to the front walk.
The gardener turns
inside to his wife, dazed, as if his hoe
had been plucked from him in mid-swing ——

MEMORY OF WHAT'S TO COME

We lived on a short street that ended in sand
and carried the smell of the sea right to our door.
We had nothing but a mattress and bad shag carpet
in a rickety beach house with the staircase
on the outside.
We were there to make love.

This simplicity
was a happy ruse:
voluptuous tears
filling my wide open eyes
at the plain sight of
pain for the sake of real love,
falling back on the bed with endless
arms surrounding and
the night opening like a long passageway
we were treading by instinct
with the future written in us
like an unremembered dream.

And no matter how early we got down to the shore —
after watching the yellow lamplight
bruise the heartbreaking purity
of daybreak —
there were already messages scraped into the
perfect slope of sand left by the tide.
It was spring and the sun was near the moon was so near
and all those things they said were true
as the ocean's scent,
mingled with the smell of cheap rental paint,
penetrated into the very planks our house was made of,
into the rug we rolled on,
into the blue hum
from the streetlights and the grit pressing up against our feet.

Right now, somewhere later in that same dream,
this scent teases my nostrils and goes straight into my brain.
We're nestled there like a foetus
and I'm putting down the words
we wrote then on the invisible slate
during every moment we made love to each other.
We are born into ourselves as into death
as into life,
into this room the size of the world
measured by everything
we can feel.

you lie also sleeping,
body of your flesh for this one life,
body of my breaking ground.
All night
a wintry wind polishes the empty streets
and when I begin crossing over at the
crack of dawn I hear your breathing.
It has been years
since I lay beside you but your conjured body
breathes beside me now
as the wind ransacks the dreams
of every sleeping soul
from here to where you
in truth lie, truly breathing, and I cry
in my painful dream and on
through the transition to consciousness
where ghost tears fill with salt
and become real on my face.

You too are dislodged
by this thrashing wind which presages winter,
I am sure of it. Winter season of sleep erasure of memory
burial for regeneration and all that,
season that sifts what's remembered into a magical
dust that never sleeps
but enters unnoticed everywhere
and changes the working of things.
This fine powder shakes itself
across your eyelids now
catalyzing the pictures shapeshifting across
the screen of your living imagination.
I am in that powder.

As dawn blooms into day
the vacuum as always tries to fill itself
with the air that is
there but the two can never
blend, nothing and something: there is no
middle ground. So the wind
keeps rushing.

On the other
side of town you might as well be
on the other side of the spinning earth
but tell me, if you can somehow hear me,
do you dream of me?
Though it's over, once a thing has happened
does it ever end?
Does your physical shape now shape
the growth of these energy fields my body?
And my body that loved you cell by cell
does it not float does it not dwell
right this minute in your corporeal body?

WHEN THE SNOW FALLS IN SUMMER

Last night the snow fell
hard in my dream
as if the sky were finally giving up the ghost.
Sky the very pinnacle of summer
inverted to winter when the snow did fall
blanketing the switching yard
grazing concrete walls on its way down
piling up in vacant lots and
making children nearby look up
in wonder and hope.

That was when we kissed goodbye for the last time.
I could stand it then,
in the beautiful snow so
pure so white so springing like
magic from a blue summer sky
but cold, so cold, I closed
my arms around him one last time.
Then open

> *I'll watch him disappear into the snowfall*
> *The world will turn white*
> *I will let go*
> *and the only sound will be the sound of snow*
> *falling on snow*

THE GIRL THAT GOT AWAY

Oh but those were real arms she held out
    as she rocked towards me over the forgetful water.
And what — what — what shall I forget —
clasping her to my heart where my own life pulses with
    the vigor of my boyhood turning to manhood
    while the sun rises steadily beyond the drawn shades?
All my sadness and all my yearning traveling from my heart
    down into her bottomless dark eyes?
Her image, dark and bright, slipping under my eyelids
    as I sleep?
Shall I forget her body swimming into my arms,
    her yielding body as I come into her, her breasts
    that make me glad? Will I?

She dives and through the lens of the water
I see her white body shifting —
then only the light glancing off the skin of the sea.

Posted like a sentry at the surface where she
    disappeared
knowing this wide ocean will never mark my hard-won
                       tears,
I realize the hush
in the burning afternoon
(the sweep of the breeze,
the waves slapping lightly against my own prow),
    the water itself sealing off the silence
        that uncloses in its depths.

THE RAIN AND THE DUST

Tender green shoots sprout in the tub of dust like pain
from any given situation.
When he took me I left, wrapping myself
in a robe of forgetfulness the size of
the memory of you, the size of summer begging for spring
   again,
and the exact texture of the way wind
disappears when still.

If it hadn't been for fear of not having I might never
have immersed myself in the kind of desire
that makes one get up and walk away from the table
and out onto a lawn of dark and endless singing stone,
swelling rain.

I made myself a prophet in order to fulfill
my own need,
a prophet of Change
shucking my clothes in the green bushes, or
sitting behind a desk in a tight dress
handing out tools marked USE THIS,
my own naked body the prophecy, the promise,

leaving you standing in a tilled field of dust trying to
invent rage but left with only fortitude,
and me, instinctively female,
inventing a tasseled curtain of rain
dark grey on the horizon, long weeks of rain
filling our eyes like empty cups,
hour after hour of rain,
forty days and forty nights
of rain, heavy barter
for such an urgent, transforming object
as desire.

GOODBYE FROM THE CITY

The sun blazes the same trail
again without leaving a mark
only darkness in its wake but before that
the glowing through the polluted horizon
turns the surface of the ocean mercurial and sliding
between pink and green the waves sliding
over each other without purpose
and the surf hushed

The sea seems to disappear into myth
as if you might glimpse the tip
of the mast of a ship bound for Lethe gone awry

And nothing will crack here it will only
suffocate and slowly burn
The conflagration on the liquid horizon
is dying, dying
No breeze, no leaves stirring
while on a heap of tar a boy sits playing
a broken taps on a trombone
not having learned yet how the music is made
and while the air is still warm with the memory of the day
the dark quickens
and the taps falls away

LITTLE SISTER SELF

I've lost her
I dreamed she flew over
the cliff

Her message
unmasked me
and after surrender
what further:

You, far away,
who are you
Sadness travels from my heart
out into my limbs
and down my untraveled path

My feet get so light I eventually feel the clouds
touch my hairline
My shoes slip off and it's a long time
before they touch the ground
I can see the trees swaying and the waves
reaching
and the grass growing up
I'm just a figment of someone's imagination
floating like a vision in the
deep blue sky
And even the colors are lifting up out of the sunrise
Money flies up and away — I let it go —
I can see below how the sand is racing
over the sand, and
flags whipping and stuttering, as if soon
to stagger up like kites —
Shopkeepers opening up shop feel
the wind tugging their hair and look up:
There's this morning's mist
rushing up from the basin
past the moveable
mountains
My feet trail below me
the stars rush above me
all sound waves
dancing upward I am
dancing too we are all dancing

DECIDUOUS

I listen to the light
coming through the leaves
is it laughing
and to the trees leaning up, finding their way
up
toward the laughter
in a kind of belly dance
so slow
you can't see they're dancing
but they are — the imperceptibly slow
dance of
growing
growing upwards
while the wild grass rolls
beneath them
through the clutter of leaves
in small billowing
upheavals of earth and seed —
Growing, growing
out to the leaf tips, which float
in their own sea of light,
and turn all
together like chimes
and hold the sky together
Growing upwards, growing so
slowly,
then slowing,
until the green decides
and draws down the cold,
the caves are exposed,
the root around the rock
writes its own world in the earth
exploring the dark
and planting downward the power
to go up,

to bear upward the imprint of leaf
via sap
— and so I see the roots dancing also
as they penetrate their breathing
space
as they mirror the branches
which embrace wind
or calm
and which form
from rain not
rain
— and I see the whole tree
giving one lifelong
shiver
which is living
itself
through which I feel the whole tree
as it is
from the roots
up
reach
without believing
into what it is

When I Miss You

Pulling into the garage I miss you
Passing the shops I miss you
Turning over in my sleep I miss you
Missing your call I miss you
Sowing my wild oats it's you I miss
Falling in love I miss you still
The fog descends and I'm missing you
The ocean turns in its sleep and I'm missing you
The light settles on the edge
   of my consciousness, again I miss you
The answers are still not there I miss you
I have stopped asking I miss you
The honey is growing
   sweeter in the nest I miss you
Iridescent as the wing
   of the blue butterfly my thoughts
   show me how I miss you
The water swirling around the edge of the island
   creeps through my bloodstream as I
   go on missing you
The strains of my own music
baffle me how I miss you — You
   are running jumping drumming
   on everything, lying restless unabating and
   green as a virgin with someone much greener
   not me, far away, unquenched and open
   as a vessel and I miss you I miss you I miss you I miss you ——

GET FREE

I'm floating
a web around his white body
For now I'll call him *x*
I'm his lover, even
the unknown neutral me I see
trapped in one of the side panels
of the 3-way mirror
thinking I'm beside myself, *yes,*
Eros will fly me out of here.

It's a soft clacking sound
the train makes
through the tall, dry night. Old One-Eye
our lone moon, so homely and
sane but with his crafty side
too, the side he never lets us
see,
looks on.
How about if the train jumps off the track
and slides instead along that groove of moonlight
cleaving the ravine?

I lay waiting for hours before
I could write this down.
Captured in a bead of water
the image of the green of grass
disappears
with evaporation —   free
And through all the measurable millenia
the spears of grass that have ever grown on Earth
add up to a finite number, making it easy to see
how freedom can mean death:
no more counting

Train whistle says lonesome,
daybreak says renewal,
moon means harvest, breast
implies succor, and so on
all the way to the bird I imagine descending from the cloud
    layer
to hover at my shoulder:
let go

TAKE A MOMENT

The sun pulls from the stone
and flits like an airplane shadow across the ground of
                                consciousness.
All I know for sure I've given up, and the sun rides me now
as if I have a choice,
or as if some flute player got hold of an instrument
and then the notes dropped to the ground
and no one knew.

At the same time I watch the leaves turn
helplessly, same as my delirium.
At the base of the fence the slats have soaked up
so much decaying power that
their rotting will be just as beautifully
helpless and mercifully forgotten
as the flash of autumn's unsigned-up members.

What if the leaves don't drop but just stay there,
what if the last time the sun enters the stone it stays,
unanswered and not groping,
what if then you step over the notes
and under the plane
and some poem catches you and slips
all your marbles to me.

Here is where we disappeared.
One minute we were flitting over
the static sun;
then the poem ended
(and no one remembered, no one).

THE PUPIL

Black curved
hole for light
but heavier
than light
and not exactly deep
    but inside
draws eyesight
inward.
See three eyes where the two
are equal
to the sum of all they've
seen but the third —
    inside
When you crank your big
head around they blur
in the transparent obsidian all charged
with itself
Thinking chases
itself like unfulfilled
electrons into
a rushing
without sound but not
silence —
while like a lantern in a window the glint
of center
    (surrounded
    by the bitter beauty of
    confusion/sensation
    and far-fetching
    helplessness of savagery
    in the soul's leonine refusal
    to tame
        (Stillness)
    burning out crystallized fuel
    and thrusting that coughing fire

out into the swirling
churning airless all
where the slightest *if*
emits non-centuries of messages
that come whispering down like ashes around your ears
which long do they not
for communing with what we can
if not see then hear)
beckons
and the sum turns on its ear

That star looks as if it's going to fall
right into the lap of the moon: luck, inconstancy.
Because of this and of chimes moving barely
on the change in the air that comes with dusk
signalling peace
I can feel everything
is going to be all right.
I can hear the buzz of eternity
in the engine of that airplane overhead, way
way up.

FINALLY THE RAIN

Hearing the rain at last, I stepped out and saw the dark day
and the rain falling in the bushes and trees,
sealing the ivy-enclosed yard, and I saw
how the thick cluster of white blossoms
trembled on the end of their
heavily laden stem,
gathering raindrops into their fragrant crevices and
                                              overflowing,
and beyond the garden stretched a green field
blurred by rain
and the music that had filled my head when I was inside
faded and disappeared
as I stood under the dripping leaves
and watched the rain fall into the still and open-armed day.

ALMOST PRESCIENT

These long nights spent awake, awake,
not lonely, not that exactly,
but when the unshapen world of what's to come
alerts me with soft untraceable noises
and I picture the dream river
glistening somehow in the dark
as it runs darkly on
then I know there is no such thing as arrival
Out in the dark a bough taps lightly against my windowpane

SISTER OF ICARUS

Escaping the house of dim, gilt-
framed portraits, gleaming oak floors, and silent heirlooms
was a matter of life and death.
The world slanted steeply as she made her way
across the third-floor bedroom, stepped onto
the windowsill and out
onto thin air.

Twilight floated her
into the powerful upper branches of the lofty elm
that had always made an axis,
and from there she thought she could glimpse
the generative aspect of black, way high up.

Her husband strode onto the well-tended lawn below,
white ascot glinting in the dusk,
calling up to her
Come down.
His distant, arcing voice
fell on deaf ears. She set off.

Propelling yourself through the earth's
gravity field is work:
if you strive too vertically you
plummet to the ground, and she landed in a heap there now.
His footsteps pounded toward her over the rich sod
and she launched herself again, working her arms in a breast
    stroke,
climbing up over the streets of her town,
up where she could see
the stars. Where?
Below her husband tracked her still by car, bearing down
on the sparkling reflection of her
diamonds on the street.

She pressed upward alone in a fine film of sweat
feeling only how dark and vast it grew.
Then what was it brushing
her cheeks and arms as lightly
as breath, except her community's prayers hurrying upward
and leaving her far behind.
Her pupils widened to a new calibre
and the dark flooded in, drew her into
its lap, and she knew she would never be
able to get back.

Before dissociating completely
she reached up and plucked
a stone from the rude ground
of the moon, and as if it were her body
let it drop through uncertainty
all the way down
to the dark, velvety lawn
where it landed with a normal sound.
Her husband was in bed, dreaming
of a lunar eclipse
when it touched ground, making him lift
his head from the pillow to let her
death in.

DREAM OF THE BIG BANG

The wood is glistening with raindrops.
Dark and light
go exchanging places through the trees.
Pine and spruce needles cushion my slow soft footfalls.
Holding up
in the vibrating silence I pick up a murmuring
voice swimming near:
My estranged sister other sister who shares a mermaid's tail
with me drifts alongside me, rocking a little and
breathing coded messages: all I can make out is
Dear me — like the salutation of a letter
of confession. I want her to speak all the way out,
but she is secretness
even to herself.

It's when we stop trying
to decipher anything that we catch sight
of the path diving off down a steep bank of the forest —
so impossibly steep, so gleaming and slippery wet
the only way to follow it
would be to fly —

but I'm beguiled by how the trees are shining with secrets,
                                    with mystery,
how meaning is everywhere, on the tips of our tongues,
and it's when we both go to power a deep stroke
of the tail at the same time and glide
through light dodging
and tree shadows
that I start to wonder if I can bring
myself to now know that the truth
is hidden invisibly in the air I breathe
and that this body I half share with my sis is
about to be born into knowledge the droplets
of which are swerving all around me —

when all at once we're flying forward at the speed of light
and we bust through a glass door the size of
everything I can see and it shatters into a million stars ——

NOTES

Solutio and *sublimatio* are Latin terms for the alchemical processes based on dissolving and evaporation.

In the poem "Without Thinking #2," the line "Rumble and gasp of the surf" is quoted from Ross Macdonald.

"Fool's Journey" and "The Pupil" are extracted from a dialogue in poetry conducted with Bill Epes. In accordance with the method of the exchange, I lifted the line "I knew a boy well who nearly found his own" from his poem #3, and the line "black/curved liquid hole for light" from his poem #5, to create my responses.

Singer, songwriter, poet and spoken-word artist, multimedia producer and performer, Carrington MacDuffie has been writing seriously since she could write. A native New Yorker, she studied literature and the arts at Johns Hopkins, Harvard, and Boston University, where she was awarded the Undergraduate Poetry Prize. Her work has been published in literary journals internationally, and she is Poetry Editor of the journal *Square Lake*.

Ms. MacDuffie has sung and recited on many stages in New York, Los Angeles, and the Pacific Northwest, and she has kept afloat as an artist by working at such various professions as paperback fiction editor, performance model, fashion stylist, freelance writer, vaudeville performer, and composer/producer. She currently makes her living as a voiceover artist, specializing in narrating audiobooks.

In collaboration with composer Bryan Nall, she has written and produced *Lunacy Dewpoint*, a CD of ambient music and spoken word drawn from poems in ON THE DREAMING EARTH. In all her work she is a devotee of the transformative energies of the imagination.